By God's Grace

VOLUME I

Gateway International, Inc.
Tulsa, Oklahoma

Unless otherwise indicated, all Scripture quotations are taken from the *King James Version* of the Bible.

By God's Grace — Volume I
Copyright © 1997 by K & C International, Inc.
ISBN 0-9632354-5-1 (Lexitone Burgundy)

Published by Gateway International
P.O. Box 702008
Tulsa, Oklahoma 74170
(918) 747-5009

CONTENTS

INTRODUCTION

Everything we are and have as believers is by God's grace. The Apostle Paul wrote, "For by grace are ye saved through faith: and that not of yourselves: it is the gift of God: Not of works, lest any man should boast" (Eph. 2:8-9). It is by His grace that we enter the Christian life, and it is by His grace that we are able to obey Him and follow through in every area of our commitment to Him. Truly, His grace is sufficient for us. (See 2 Cor. 12:9.)

This book is about the Lord's all-sufficient grace at work in our lives. *By God's Grace* is a devotional resource designed to help you to focus on the truth of God's Word of grace which, as Jesus declares, "shall make you free" (John 8:32). Grace and truth — key elements in finding spiritual freedom and victory — are presented from a unique, user-friendly perspective on each page of this book by way of biblical material in the form of personal commitments, key Scriptures, relevant quotations and sayings, related Scriptures, Word-based prayers, and faith-filled affirmations. Your life will change as you meditate upon the truths of God's Word and claim His promises for your life.

This is not a book of rules, regulations, and laws. Rather, it is a book of love and grace that reveals the Father's great care and mercy in your life. God wants you to live a happy, fulfilled life in accordance with His plans and purposes for you, and trustful obedience to His Word is an important means of receiving His grace that enables you to do so.

Jesus said, "If ye love me, keep my commandments" (John 14:15). Clearly, God expects us to walk according to His commandments because He loves us. By His grace, and through obedience to His Word, we are able to receive His love and demonstrate our love for Him.

God gives us principles, guidelines, and commandments that will make our journey more joyful and complete. As we reflect upon God's precepts, as they are outlined in the pages of this book — a series of *By God's Grace* commitments, followed by key Scriptures — we grow in faith and become ever-more determined to obey our loving Father.

It is important to realize that the power to fulfill each commitment comes from the indwelling presence of the Lord in our lives. "I am the vine, ye are the branches: He that abideth in me, and I in him, the same bringeth forth much fruit: for without me ye can do nothing" (John 15:5).

You will find each page of this book to be a stepping-stone to greater joy, health, growth, and victory through Jesus Christ, your Lord. Memorize His Word and let it have full course in your life. This will keep you from sin, as the Psalmist declared, "Thy word have I hid in mine heart, that I might not sin against thee"

(Ps. 119:11). The powerful Word of God is sharper than any two-edged sword. It is, in fact, the sword of the Spirit that enables you to defeat the enemy in all areas of your life.

By God's grace you will be able to take your stand on the Word as you covenant with God in each area of personal commitment. He will supply you with all the grace and power you will need to win the battle in each area of your life. You can depend upon His Word.

Our prayer is that, as you examine your problems in the light of the Word, you will see everything from an entirely new perspective. We pray that you will know that you will never again participate in any of the unfruitful works of darkness because your life is rooted and grounded in the Word, and God's grace is entirely sufficient for you.

*F*or by grace are ye saved through faith: and that not of yourselves: it is the gift of God: Not of works, lest any man should boast.

*T*rust in the Lord with all thine heart; and lean not unto thine own understanding. In all thy ways acknowledge him, and he shall direct thy paths.

Proverbs 3:5-6

ANGER

Commitment: By God's grace I will never again be angry without good cause.

Scripture for Today: *"Wherefore, my beloved brethren, let every man be swift to hear, slow to speak, slow to wrath: For the wrath of man worketh not the righteousness of God"* (James 1:19-20).

Quote of the Day: "Anger is only one letter short of danger" (Anonymous).

Meditation: Billy Graham said, "Nothing is ever solved by hot heads and cold hearts." Throughout this day I will endeavor to "keep my cool" and to keep coming from love, warmth, and forgiveness in all my relationships and responsibilities. I will learn how to deal with my anger in positive, constructive, and proactive ways because I know this is God's will for me. He tells me to overcome my anger by being kind and tender-hearted toward others. (See Eph. 4:32.)

Related Scriptures: *Proverbs 15:18; Proverbs 16:32; Proverbs 19:11; Proverbs 27:4; Matthew 5:22; Ephesians 4:26.*

Prayer: Heavenly Father, keep me from destructive anger, and teach me how to handle all my feelings in your perfect way. I will forgive others as you have forgiven me.

Affirmation: I will deal with my anger in positive ways because I know it is a God-given emotion that leads me to positive changes.

AUTHORITY

Commitment: By God's grace I will never again question the Lord's authority.

Scripture for Today: *"Woe unto him that striveth with his Maker! Let the potsherd strive with the potsherds of the earth. Shall the clay say to him that fashioneth it, What makest thou? or thy work, He hath no hands?"* (Isaiah 45:9).

Quote of the Day: "God moves in a mysterious way — His wonders to perform" (William Cowper).

Meditation: My heavenly Father is all-powerful and all-knowing. He knows what I need even before I express it to Him. (See Matt. 6:8.) God knows what is best for me. How big is my God? He is big enough to satisfy all the longings of my soul! I know that my Father — almighty

God — will supply all my needs according to His riches in glory. (See Phil. 4:19.)

Related Scriptures: *Psalms 18:30; Proverbs 3:5-6; Isaiah 45:18; Revelation 19:6.*

Prayer: Father, forgive me for ever questioning your authority in my life. I truly know that all things do work together for good in my life. I love you, and I know you have called me and chosen me to be your child. Thank you for your matchless love.

Affirmation: Jesus is my Lord!

CONFIDENCE

Commitment: By God's grace I will never again put my confidence in my own ability.

Scripture for Today: *"Trust in the Lord with all thine heart; and lean not unto thine own understanding. In all thy ways acknowledge him, and he shall direct thy paths"* (Proverbs 3:5-6).

Quote of the Day: "My strength is as the strength of ten, because my heart is pure" (Alfred, Lord Tennyson).

Meditation: In quietness and in confidence I find great strength. (See Isa. 30:15.) I will trust in the Lord throughout this day, and I know He will fight my battles for me. (See 2 Chron. 32:8.) The confidence I have in Him assures me that He will hear and answer my prayers.

(See 1 John 5:14-15.) I will trust in Him at all times instead of leaning on my worldly understanding, and I know He will direct my paths. Jesus never fails.

Related Scriptures: *2 Chronicles 32:8; Psalms 20:7; Psalms 118:8; Proverb 3:26; Proverbs 25:19; Philippians 3:3.*

Prayer: Dear Lord, I know you as my personal Savior and Lord. Thank you for all you are accomplishing in my life. You are enabling me to do every good work in your name. I can do all things through you.

Affirmation: I will trust in the Lord with all my heart.

DEPRESSION

Commitment: By God's grace I will never again give in to depression.

Scripture for Today: *"Why art thou cast down, O my soul? and why art thou disquieted within me? hope in God: for I shall yet praise him, who is the health of my countenance, and my God"* (Ps. 43:5).

Quote of the Day: "Every thing that is done in the world is done by hope" (Martin Luther).

Meditation: Though the devil seeks to discourage me, and circumstances sometimes threaten to overwhelm me, I will hold on to my faith, hope, and confidence in God. I will not choose to live under any negative circumstance, because I know that emotions are not my lord and circumstances are not my master. I choose to be the head, not the tail, and I will walk by faith, not by sight. (See 2 Cor. 5:7.) I will remember that no weapon that is formed against me shall prosper, and every tongue that rises against me in judgment will be condemned. (See Isa. 54:17.) These facts of my faith lift me out of depression, for "This is the heritage of the servants of the Lord" (Isa. 54:17).

Related Scriptures: *Psalms 34:18-19; Psalms 103:1-2; Psalms 147:3.*

Prayer: Heavenly Father, thank you for blessing me in so many important ways. I will walk in your blessing by focusing on your promises rather than my problems. In so doing, I know you will lead me out of depression, into the sunshine of your love.

Affirmation: I will praise God with all my heart.

FAITH

Commitment: By God's grace I will never worry again.

Scripture for Today: *"Be careful for nothing; but in every thing by prayer and supplication with thanksgiving let your requests be made known unto God. And the peace of God, which passeth all understanding, shall keep your hearts and minds through Christ Jesus"* (Phil. 4:6-7).

Quote of the Day: "Worry is the interest paid on trouble before it is due" (Anonymous).

Meditation: Jesus cares about me, and He wants me to cast all of my cares upon Him. (See 1 Pet. 5:7.) I willingly let go of my worries as I do the best I can with the situations that confront me this day. As I do my best, I know God will do the rest. He has already given me a peace that surpasses understanding. (See Phil. 4:6-7.) Throughout this day, I will put God first, and I know He will take care of the things I cannot change. (See Matt. 6:33.) Realizing that a key to greater strength is found in the quiet mind, I will live in each subsequent present moment instead of borrowing trouble from the future through worry.

Related Scriptures: *Isaiah 26:3; John 14:1; John 14:27; Colossians 3:15; 1 Peter 5:7.*

Prayer: Lord God, I know you do not want me to worry at all. I believe your Word which promises me that you will not withhold any good thing from those who love you. I love you, Lord.

Affirmation: I will walk in peace throughout this day, because I know God is taking care of me. Great is His faithfulness in my life.

FEAR

Commitment: By God's grace I will never again fear death.

Scripture for Today: *"Verily, verily, I say unto you, He that believeth on me hath everlasting life"* (John 6:47).

Quote of the Day: "The fear of God kills all other fears" (Hugh Black).

Meditation: Some people are afraid of death, but since I met Jesus I've realized that death has no power over me at all. "For the wages of sin is death; but the gift of God is eternal life through Jesus Christ our Lord" (Rom. 6:23). "Fear," as George MacDonald wrote, "is faithlessness." I choose to believe God, and He promises that, "Surely goodness and mercy shall follow me all the days of my life: and I will dwell in the house of the Lord for ever" (Ps. 23:6).

Related Scriptures: *John 3:16; John 4:14; John 5:24; John 6:47; John 6:51; John 10:27-28; John 11:25-26; 1 Corinthians 15:54-55; Hebrews 2:14-15.*

Prayer: Lord, thank you for erasing my fear of death by the victory of Jesus' resurrection. Because He lives, I can face all my tomorrows without fear.

Affirmation: Jesus is the Resurrection and the Life.

GOD'S WILL

Commitment: By God's grace I will never again refuse to follow the Lord's will.

Scripture for Today: *"Commit thy works unto the Lord, and thy thoughts shall be established"* (Prov. 16:3).

Quote of the Day: "If you abide in the will of God, you will have an experience that will abide" (Anonymous).

Meditation: God's way is perfect. (See Ps. 18:30.) Therefore, I will trust in His Word which reveals His will to me. I will rejoice evermore and pray without ceasing as I give thanks in everything, because I know this is God's will for me. (See 1 Thess. 5:16-18.) God wants only the best for me at all times, and this is why He has given me guidelines to live by. His Word is "a lamp unto my feet, and a light unto my path" (Ps. 119:105). I will walk in the lamplight, along the path He has set before me. I choose His will over my own in the same way Jesus did in the Garden of Gethsemane: "Nevertheless not my will, but thine, be done" (Luke 22:42). I know His will is always best.

Related Scriptures: *Psalms 48:14; Psalms 119; Proverbs 3:5-6; Proverbs 16:3; Isaiah 30:21; Isaiah 58:11.*

Prayer: Lord God, I know your will for me is always good. I want your will to become my will, your thoughts to be my thoughts, your ways to be my ways. I accept your will and determine to walk in it throughout this day.

Affirmation: The will of God — nothing more, nothing less, nothing else.

GOD'S WORD

Commitment: By God's grace I will never again avoid the study of the Word.

Scripture for Today: *"I will delight myself in thy statutes: I will not forget thy word"* (Ps. 119:16).

Quote of the Day: "Many possess the Bible; too few are possessed by it" (Anonymous).

Meditation: I love the Word of God. It provides me with life, direction, wisdom, and understanding. I will let it live in my mind, my heart, my soul. I will cherish its promises, and translate its message into my life today. I will take delight in meditating upon its truth. I will stand upon it, and let its faith fill my life. I will search the Scriptures, and study to show myself approved unto

God so that I will be a workman who never needs to be ashamed. (See 2 Tim. 2:15.) I will remember what Billy Graham said, "Our faith is not dependent upon human knowledge and scientific advance, but upon the unmistakable message of the Word of God."

Related Scriptures: *Psalms 119:9; Psalms 119:11; Psalms 119:47; Psalms 119:89; Psalms 119:93; Psalms 119:130; Psalms 119:160; 2 Timothy 2:15; 2 Timothy 3:16.*

Prayer: Thank you for your Word, Lord. It is a lamp unto my feet and a light unto my path. I will stand and walk upon your Word today.

Affirmation: I will let God speak to me through His Word today.

GRACE

Commitment: By God's grace I will never exchange His grace for the Law.

Scripture for Today: *"I do not frustrate the grace of God: for if righteousness come by the law, then Christ is dead in vain"* (Gal. 2:21).

Quote of the Day: "There is nothing but God's grace. We walk upon it; we breath it; we live and die by it" (Robert Louis Stevenson).

Meditation: Jonathan Edwards wrote, "Grace is but glory begun, and glory is but grace perfected." I owe everything in my spiritual life to the work of grace, because I have never deserved any of God's blessings. My Father is a gracious God who loves to give and give and give. This truly is grace's prerogative — to give and give and give. My life in

Christ began with a work of grace: "For by grace are ye saved through faith; and that not of yourselves: it is the gift of God. Not of works, lest any man should boast" (Eph. 2:8-9). His amazing grace sustains me still.

Related Scriptures: *Romans 8:28; Galatians 3:24-26; Ephesians 2:8-9.*

Prayer: Thank you, Lord, for your marvelous grace that enables me to enjoy every spiritual blessing in Christ Jesus.

Affirmation: God's grace is greater than all my sin.

GROWTH

Commitment: By God's grace I will never again forget to seek the Lord.

Scripture for Today: *"Seek the Lord, and his strength: seek his face evermore"* (Ps. 105:4).

Quote of the Day: "Begin to know Him now, and finish never" (Oswald Chambers).

Meditation: Hannah Whitall Smith wrote, "The mother eagle teaches her little ones to fly by making their nest so uncomfortable that they are forced to leave it and commit themselves to the unknown world of air outside. And just so does our God to us. He stirs up our comfortable nests, and pushes us over the edge of them, and we are forced to use our wings to save ourselves from fatal falling. Read your trials in this light, and see if you cannot begin to get a glimpse of their meaning. Your wings are being developed."

Related Scriptures: *Psalms 27:8; Isaiah 55:6; Matthew 6:33.*

Prayer: Heavenly Father, I put you first in my life, and I will seek you in every experience of this day. Thank you for always being the God who is there.

Affirmation: "Wise men still seek Him" (Anonymous).

HEALTH AND HEALING

Commitment: By God's grace I will never again eat foods that are harmful to me.

Scripture for Today: *"And they that are Christ's have crucified the flesh with the affections and lusts"* (Gal. 5:24).

Quote of the Day: "The mouth has a little hole, but it can swallow house and roof" (Yiddish proverb).

Meditation: This is the day when I will begin to practice moderation in all things, especially with regard to my food intake. God has promised to supply all my needs (See Phil. 4:19), so I will be satisfied with eating only what I truly need. I will avoid all foods that are not good for me, and that will cause me to gain weight. One fruit of the Spirit of

God in my life is temperance, and I want to bear that fruit throughout this day. Self-control under the control of my Master will keep me from the sin of gluttony.

Related Scriptures: *Romans 8:5; Romans 8:6-8; Galatians 5:22-23; Galatians 5:25.*

Prayer: Lord, I ask for your help in keeping my appetite under control today. Your empowering presence enables me to eat only those things that are good for me.

Affirmation: I will choose the foods I eat very carefully.

HOLINESS

Commitment: By God's grace I will never again allow myself to be conformed to the ways of this world.

Scripture for Today: *"Set your affection on things above, not on things on the earth"* (Col. 3:2).

Quote of the Day: "Be pure as snow, but don't drift" (Anonymous).

Meditation: God's standard is holiness. It is written, "Follow peace with all men, and holiness, without which no man shall see the Lord" (Heb. 12:14). I will walk in holiness today, remembering the words of Oswald Chambers who said, "If we are going to retain personal contact with the Lord Jesus Christ, it will mean there are some things we must scorn to do or to think, some legitimate things we must scorn to touch." I am clothed with the righteousness of Christ, and He will fill me with His Spirit. (See Eph. 5:18.)

Related Scriptures: *Romans 6:11-12; Romans 12:1-2; Ephesians 5:11.*

Prayer: Father, thank you for Jesus who is my righteousness and my holiness. Through Him, I am able to be perfect even as you are perfect. (See Matt. 5:48.)

Affirmation: I'd rather have Jesus than anything else.

HOLY SPIRIT

Commitment: By God's grace I will never again choose to walk in the flesh instead of the Spirit.

Scripture for Today: *"If we live in the Spirit, let us also walk in the Spirit"* (Gal. 5:25).

Quote of the Day: "No power on earth or in hell can conquer the Spirit of God in a human spirit. It is an inner inconquerableness" (Oswald Chambers).

Meditation: Samuel Chadwick wisely observed, "It is the Spirit that quickens. Everything else fails. The letter may be faultlessly orthodox, the method may be marvelously ingenious, the man may be tremendously earnest, but only the God-made, God-inspired, God-enabled avails. The Power that quickly transforms, perfects, is the God of the Spirit." I will be filled with God's Spirit today, and only in this way will I be able to live a life that reflects the character and holiness of God, my Father.

Related Scriptures: *Romans 8:1; Romans 8:14.*

Prayer: Father, fill me with your Spirit so that I will be able to produce the fruit of your Spirit in all the relationships and responsibilities of my life today.

Affirmation: God, the Spirit, dwells in me!

INTERCESSION

Commitment: By God's grace I will never again fail to intercede for those in leadership.

Scripture for Today: *"I exhort therefore, that, first of all, supplications, prayers, intercessions, and giving of thanks, be made for all men; For kings, and for all that are in authority; that we may lead a quiet and peaceable life in all godliness and honesty. For this is good and acceptable in the sight of God our Saviour"* (1 Tim. 2:1-3).

Quote of the Day: "Prayer is a sincere, sensible, affectionate pouring out of the soul to God, through Christ in the strength and assistance of the Spirit, for such things as God has promised" (John Bunyan).

Meditation: "Let every soul be subject unto the higher powers. For there is no power but of God: the powers that be are ordained of God" (Rom. 13:1). Those who are in authority over me are blessings of God — gifts from God that help me to live my life quietly and peaceably. Because this is true, I will be certain to pray for government officials, church leaders, employers, supervisors, and all those I have the privilege of serving. I understand how much they need my prayer support, and I will pray for them daily.

Related Scriptures: *2 Chronicles 7:14; Romans 13:1.*

Prayer: Father, I thank you for calling me by your name. I humble myself in prayer, seeking your face. I repent of my sins, and I pray for those in authority over me: _____

_____.

Affirmation: I will "stand in the gap" in behalf of all those in authority over me.

JESUS

Commitment: By God's grace I will never again forget what Jesus did for me when He saved me.

Scripture for Today: *"But God commendeth his love toward us, in that, while we were yet sinners, Christ died for us"* (Rom. 5:8).

Quote of the Day: "Christ is not valued at all unless He is valued above all" (St. Augustine).

Meditation: Jesus is my way, my truth, my life. (See John 14:6.) Without Him, I can do nothing. (See John 15:5.) The words "believe on the Lord Jesus Christ" mean "to have an absolute personal reliance upon the Lord Jesus Christ." I realize that I am totally dependent upon Him. It is He who has saved me from my sin, my self, my struggles, and my fears. He is my light in the darkness, my joy in sadness, my riches in poverty, and my life in death. I love the Lord. He is my Savior and King.

Related Scriptures: *Luke 1:47; Luke 19:10; John 3:16; John 6:47; Ephesians 2:8-9; Romans 3:23; Romans 6:23.*

Prayer: Father, thank you for sending Jesus to be the propitiation for my sins. (See 1 John 2:2.) His blood cleanses me from all my sins. (See 1 John 1:7.)

Affirmation: Jesus is my answer, no matter what the question.

JOY

Commitment: By God's grace I will never again quench the joy of the Lord in my life or the lives of others.

Scripture for Today: *"The joy of the Lord is your strength"* (Neh. 8:10).

Quote of the Day: "Fun is natural pleasure; joy is spiritual pleasure" (Anonymous).

Meditation: The joy God gives goes beyond happiness, fun, and pleasure. It is thoroughly spiritual, not emotional. It involves gladness, delight, a state of gratitude. Even in moments of tribulation and upheaval, it is possible for me to experience the joy of the Lord which is my strength. (See Neh. 8:10.) This kind of joy does not deny the tears of loss, but it sees beyond the tears — to the ultimate triumph of our Lord and Savior Jesus Christ. He wants my joy to be full, and that is why He pours His grace upon me.

Related Scriptures: *Psalms 51:12; Psalms 118:24; Proverbs 17:22; John 15:11; Romans 14:17.*

Prayer: Lord, thank you for the fullness of joy that you have imparted to me. I will walk in joy throughout this day.

Affirmation: The joy of the Lord is my strength.

JUDGING

Commitment: By God's grace I will never again judge others with a critical spirit.

Scripture for Today: *"Brethren, if a man be overtaken in a fault, ye which are spiritual, restore such an one in the spirit of meekness; considering thyself, lest thou also be tempted"* (Gal. 6:1).

Quote of the Day: "Two things are bad for the heart — running away in fear and running down people" (Anonymous).

Meditation: As I recognize how much I need God's forgiveness in my life each day, I realize more fully that my responsibility to others is not to judge them, but to love them, confront them, and help them. The Scriptures say, "Owe no man any thing, but to love one

42

another: for he that loveth another hath fulfilled the law" (Rom. 13:8). I will take a good look at my own life today, minding my own business, and seeking all God has for me. I will speak the truth in love to those I recognize to be struggling (See Eph. 4:15) in an effort to help them through constructive criticism.

Related Scriptures: *Matthew 5:22-24; Matthew 7:1-4.*

Prayer: Father, help me to see others as you see them, and to receive others as you have received me. (See Rom. 15:7.) Show me how I might encourage other people in you instead of dragging them down.

Affirmation: I will be a blessing to other people today and always.

KINDNESS

Commitment: By God's grace I will never again forget to bear the fruit of kindness in my life.

Scripture for Today: *"Put on therefore, as the elect of God, holy and beloved, bowels of mercies, kindness, humbleness of mind, meekness, longsuffering"* (Col. 3:12).

Quote of the Day: "I expect to pass through life but once. If, therefore, there be any kindness I can show, or any good thing I can do to any fellow being, let me do it now, for I shall not pass this way again" (William Penn).

Meditation: There is no excuse for a lack of kindness on my part. I will live according to the Golden Rule which commands me to treat others as I would like them to treat me. Because I like to be treated kindly I will be sure to practice kindness toward others. I will look for creative, new ways to be kind — in both my words and actions. I will remember the words of Joseph Joubert who said, "Kindness consists in loving people more than they deserve." This was the type of kindness God extended to me when I was a sinner. "But God commendeth his love toward us, in that, while we were yet sinners, Christ died for us" (Rom. 5:8).

Related Scriptures: *2 Corinthians 6:6; 2 Peter 1:7-8.*

Prayer: Father, empower me to be kind at all times to everyone with whom I come in contact. I will look for ways to express kindness at all times.

Affirmation: I will do as many kindnesses as possible today.

LOVE

Commitment: By God's grace I will never stop loving the Lord with all my heart, soul, and strength.

Scripture for Today: *"And thou shalt love the Lord thy God with all thy heart, and with all thy soul, and with all thy mind, and with all thy strength"* (Mark 12:30).

Quote of the Day: "You will find as you look back upon your life that the moments when you have really lived are the moments when you have done things in the spirit of love" (Henry Drummond).

Meditation: The Scripture says, "We love him, because he first loved us" (1 John 4:19). The context of this truth is a passage about the supremacy of love in which the Apostle John writes, "There is no fear in love; but perfect love casteth out fear: because fear hath torment. He that feareth is not made perfect in love" (1 John 4:18). I am able to walk in love throughout this day because I know God loves me. His magnificent love is deeper than the ocean, wider than the sea, higher than Mt. Everest, and greater than the universe. Truly it compels me to surrender all that I am and have to God who is love. (See 1 John 4:8.)

Related Scriptures: *John 14:21; 1 John 4.*

Prayer: Father, fill me with your love so that I will be able to love everyone I meet today. Thank you for your love which sets me totally free from myself, my fears, and my insecurities.

Affirmation: God is love!

MERCY

Commitment: By God's grace I will never again forget God's mercies to me.

Scripture for Today: *"I beseech you therefore, brethren, by the mercies of God, that ye present your bodies a living sacrifice, holy, acceptable unto God, which is your reasonable service. And be not conformed to this world: but be ye transformed by the renewing of your mind, that ye may prove what is that good, and acceptable, and perfect, will of God"* (Rom. 12:1-2).

Quote of the Day: "Mercy is like the rainbow, which God hath set in the clouds; it never shines after it is night. If we refuse mercy here, we shall have justice in eternity" (Jeremy Taylor).

Meditation: God has been so merciful to me throughout my life. As I reflect on His mercies to me, I am filled with a sense of wonder and gratitude that motivates me to present my entire life to Him. I want to be used by Him in service and ministry. Therefore, I will not allow myself to be conformed to this world in any way whatsoever — in my thoughts, motives, or behaviors. I will transform my mind by washing in the water of God's Word every day. (See Eph. 5:26.) In this way I will prove and live out God's good, acceptable, and perfect will for my life.

Related Scriptures: *Exodus 34:6-7; Job 10:12; Hebrews 4:16.*

Prayer: Teach me, O Lord, to feel the pain and needs of others in the same way you have understood me. Let me show mercy to others in the same way you have rained your mercy upon me.

Affirmation: I will do justly, love mercy, and walk humbly with my God. (See Mic. 6:8.)

MIRACLES

Commitment: By God's grace I will never again doubt the Lord's miracle-working power.

Scripture for Today: *"Rabbi, we know that thou art a teacher come from God: for no man can do these miracles that thou doest, except God be with him"* (John 3:2).

Quote of the Day: "The Age of Miracles is forever here!" (Thomas Carlyle).

Meditation: On July 21, 1925, at the trial of teacher John Scopes, in Dayton, Tennessee, the prosecuting attorney, William Jennings Bryan, said, "One miracle is just as easy to believe as another." He was referring to the miracle of creation. One look at the world around us teaches us that the Age of Miracles is still upon us — a rose opening its petals to the sun, an infidel turning to Jesus Christ, the birth of a baby, a sick person made well — all these are miracles that supersede the ordinary. Jesus Christ, my Lord and Savior, is the same yesterday, today, and tomorrow. (See Heb. 13:8.)

Related Scriptures: *Numbers 14:21-22; John 3:2; John 12:37; Acts 15:11-12.*

Prayer: Father, I believe you can do anything. Nothing is impossible for you. (See Luke 1:37.) Thank you for your miracle-working power.

Affirmation: I believe in the God of miracles.

MONEY

Commitment: By God's grace I will never again love money.

Scripture for Today: *"For the love of money is the root of all evil: which while some coveted after, they have erred from the faith, and pierced themselves through with many sorrows. But thou, O man of God, flee these things; and follow after righteousness, godliness, faith, love, patience, meekness"* (1 Tim. 6:10-11).

Quote of the Day: "Money is an article which may be used as a universal passport to everywhere except heaven, and as a universal provider of everything except happiness" (Anonymous).

Meditation: We cannot take our money with us; therefore, it is advisable for us to do as Jesus commanded, "Lay not up for yourselves treasures upon earth, where moth and rust doth corrupt, and where thieves break through and steal: For where your treasure is, there will your heart be also" (Matt. 6:20-21).

Related Scriptures: *Psalms 122:6; Proverbs 11:28; Luke 12:15; 1 Timothy 6:17-18.*

Prayer: Heavenly Father, thank you for all the material possessions you have given to me. I will use them, and the money I earn, to serve you.

Affirmation: I will control my money instead of letting my money control me.

NEWNESS OF LIFE

Commitment: By God's grace I will never again forget to walk in newness of life.

Scripture for Today: *"Therefore we are buried with him by baptism into death: that like as Christ was raised up from the dead by the glory of the Father, even so we also should walk in newness of life"* (Rom. 6:4).

Quote of the Day: "The man who walks with God always gets to his destination" (Anonymous).

Meditation: The early church had a simple creed: "Jesus Christ is Lord." Either Jesus is Lord of all in my life or He is not Lord at all. I crown Him the Lord of lords and King of kings in my life as I endeavor to walk in newness of life in the here-and-now. As I give Him the reigns of my life, I know He will renew my life. "Knowing this, that our old man is crucified with him, that the body of sin might be destroyed, that henceforth we should not serve sin. For he that is dead is freed from sin" (Rom. 6:6-7). Because I know this is true, I reckon myself to be dead indeed unto sin, "but alive unto God through Jesus Christ our Lord" (Rom. 6:11).

Related Scriptures: *Romans 6:4; Romans 6:6-7; Romans 6:11; Romans 7:6.*

Prayer: Father, I thank you that you have justified me through faith. (See Rom. 3:28.) You have made all things new in my life. (See Rev. 21:5.)

Affirmation: I am a new creation in Christ Jesus, my Lord. (See 2 Cor. 5:17.)

OBEDIENCE

Commitment: By God's grace I will never again choose to disobey the Lord.

Scripture for Today: *"To obey is better than sacrifice, and to hearken than the fat of rams"* (1 Sam. 15:22).

Quote of the Day: "Obedience to God is the most infallible evidence of sincere and supreme love to Him" (Nathanael Emmons).

Meditation: Obedience is a choice that is up to me. I choose either to obey or to disobey. I always want to obey my Lord, and I know He gives me the strength to do so. Jesus said, "If ye love me, keep my commandments" (John 14:15). I do love Him, and I choose to obey Him in everything. I believe the words of Frederick William Robertson who wrote, "It has been well remarked, it is not said that after keeping God's commandments, but in keeping them there is great reward. God has linked these two things together, and no man can separate them — obedience and peace."

Related Scriptures: *Deuteronomy 11:26-28; Psalms 143:10; John 14:15; John 14:21.*

Prayer: Lord, I know there is no other way to be happy in Jesus but to trust Him and to obey Him. These are my choices this very day.

Affirmation: I delight to do God's will. (See Ps. 40:8.)

PATIENCE

Commitment: By God's grace I will never again give in to impatience.

Scripture for Today: *"I waited patiently for the Lord; and he inclined unto me, and heard my cry"* (Ps. 40:1).

Quote of the Day: "He that can have patience can have what he will" (Benjamin Franklin).

Meditation: Remembering that "Rome wasn't built in a day," I will endeavor to be patient about my Christian growth, prayer life, and others around me. I realize that patience is a fruit of God's indwelling Holy Spirit in my life. (See Gal. 5:22.) Someone has observed, "Patience is a virtue, possess it if you can — seldom found in people, without God's grace to stand." Though I know such generalizations are not always accurate, I do know that I need patience in my life. Therefore, I will be filled with the Spirit so that I can bear the fruit of patience in all my responsibilities and relationships throughout this day.

Related Scriptures: *Romans 8:25; Galatians 5:22; Hebrews 6:12.*

Prayer: Lord, you have always been very patient with me. Fill me with your Spirit so that I can have patience in my life no matter what circumstances may come my way.

Affirmation: I will walk in patience today.

PEACE

Commitment: By God's grace I will never again take my mind off Jesus.

Scripture for Today: *"Thou wilt keep him in perfect peace, whose mind is stayed on thee; because he trusteth in thee"* (Isa. 26:3).

Quote of the Day: "I could not live in peace if I put the shadow of a willful sin between myself and God" (George Eliot).

Meditation: Jesus gives me His peace, and it is something so sacred and precious that the world cannot take it away. (See John 14:27.) "To be spiritually minded is life and peace" (Rom. 8:6). I choose to be spiritually minded, not carnally minded, so that I can experience and live in "the peace of God, which passeth all understanding" (Phil. 4:7). I will keep my mind stayed on God, trusting

Him unreservedly, and I know that abiding spiritual peace will be mine. I love the Word of God, and this gives me great peace as well. (See Ps. 119:165.) I will walk in peace today.

Related Scriptures: *Psalms 29:11; Psalms 119:165; John 14:27; Romans 8:6; Ephesians 2:14; Philippians 4:7.*

Prayer: Heavenly Father, thank you for Jesus who is my peace. (See Eph. 2:14.) Fill me with His Spirit so that I will bear the fruit of peace in all my relationships and responsibilities today. (See Gal. 5:22.)

Affirmation: Jesus is my peace.

POWER

Commitment: By God's grace I will never again let anything block the Lord's power in my life.

Scripture for Today: *"Finally, my brethren, be strong in the Lord, and in the power of his might"* (Eph. 6:10).

Quote of the Day: "Your weakness is no excuse: 'He giveth power to the faint'" (Anonymous). (See Isa. 40:29.)

Meditation: "The Lord is my light and my salvation; whom shall I fear? the Lord is the strength of my life; of whom shall I be afraid?" (Ps. 27:1). God's power and strength are truly available to me every day of my life. This fact keeps me from fear. God is my refuge and my strength; He is "a very present help in trouble" (Ps. 46:1). "Blessed is the man whose strength is in thee" (Ps. 84:5). Indeed, it gives me peace, joy, and happiness to know that God is my strength; therefore, I will fear no one and no thing. God is my all in all, and Jesus is everything to me.

Related Scriptures: *Psalms 27:1; Psalms 46:1; Psalms 84:5; Isaiah 40:29; Colossians 1:10-12.*

Prayer: Lord, you are my light and my salvation. You are the strength of my life. I receive your power in my life, and I know I shall prevail.

Affirmation: God is omnipotent! (See Rev. 19:6.)

PRAISE

Commitment: By God's grace I will never again cease to praise and thank my heavenly Father.

Scripture for Today: *"I will bless the Lord at all times: his praise shall continually be in my mouth"* (Ps. 34:1).

Quote of the Day: "The worship most acceptable to God comes from a thankful and cheerful heart" (Plutarch).

Meditation: I greatly appreciate the old hymn that encourages me to "Count your blessings, Name them one by one; Count your blessings, See what God hath done" (J. Oatman, Jr.). I will let praise be the theme song of my life, because I have so many things for which to be thankful. First and foremost, I am thankful for who God is — "Wonderful,

Counsellor, The mighty God, The everlasting Father, The Prince of Peace. Of the increase of his government and peace there shall be no end . . ." (Isa. 9:6-7). I am thankful, also, for all God has done for me, and I will never forget His many benefits in my life. (See Ps. 103:2.) It is so good to know the Lord.

Related Scriptures: *Psalms 9:1-2; Psalms 22:3; Psalms 33:1; Psalms 48:1; Psalms 71:8; Psalms 103:2; Isaiah 9:6-7.*

Prayer: Lord, I love you and I thank you for your countless blessings in my life. As I begin to reflect on all you have done for me, my heart swells with praise. Praise the Lord!

Affirmation: God is great, and He is greatly to be praised. (See Ps. 48:1.)

PRAYER

Commitment: By God's grace I will never again let other things keep me from experiencing the power of prayer.

Scripture for Today: *"If I regard iniquity in my heart, the Lord will not hear me"* (Ps. 66:18).

Quote of the Day: "Prayer is not the breaking down of the reluctance of God. It is taking hold of the willingness of God" (Anonymous).

Meditation: I believe in the power of prayer. Several things will keep me from getting answers to my prayers — iniquity in my heart, unbelief, disobedience, hard-heartedness, insincerity, etc. However, there are several things that, if I will practice them, will assure that my prayers will be answered. These include: (1) Faith in God as a Rewarder of all those that diligently seek Him. (See Heb. 11:6.) This kind of faith involves unwavering trust and confidence; (2) The alignment of my request with the will of God. (See 1 John 5: 14-15.); (3) Submission to the Father in all things. (See James 4:6-8.) My God is a prayer-answering Father.

Related Scriptures: *Job 35:13; Hebrews 11:6; James 4:3; James 4:6-8; 1 John 5:14-15.*

Prayer: Father, I know you hear and answer my prayers when I come to you in faith, purity of heart, and submission to your will. Teach me your ways in prayer and all other aspects of life.

Affirmation: I believe God.

PRIDE

Commitment: By God's grace I will never again give in to the pride of life.

Scripture for Today: *"Humble yourselves in the sight of the Lord, and he shall lift you up"* (James 4:10).

Quote of the Day: "Pride is the master sin of the devil" (Edwin Hubbell Chapin).

Meditation: The Book of Common Prayer provides us with a prayer for deliverance from pride: "From pride, vain-glory, and hypocrisy; from envy, hatred, and malice, and all uncharitableness, good Lord, deliver us." Realizing that pride is the master sin of the devil, I want absolutely nothing to do with it. Almost all sins stem from pride, and it is known as one of the Seven Deadly Sins. I believe God's Word which tells me, "God resisteth the proud, and giveth grace to the humble" (1 Pet. 5:5). With this truth in mind, therefore, I willingly humble myself under the mighty hand of God. (See 1 Pet. 5:6.) I need God.

Related Scriptures: *Proverbs 6:16-19; Proverbs 18:12; Proverbs 28:25; 1 Peter 5:5-6.*

Prayer: Lord, deliver me from all traces of pride and egotism. I want to be your servant at all times.

Affirmation: Humility leads to honor. (See Prov. 18:12.)

QUIETNESS

Commitment: By God's grace I will never again neglect my quiet times with the Lord.

Scripture for Today: *"In returning and rest shall ye be saved; in quietness and in confidence shall be your strength"* (Isa. 30:15).

Quote of the Day: "The silent man is often worth listening to" (Anonymous).

Meditation: In times of quiet I can hear the voice of the Lord speaking to me. I will seek such quiet times of worship, prayer, meditation, and listening. Jesus said, "I am the good shepherd, and know my sheep, and am known of mine" (John 10:14), then He went on to say, "My sheep hear my voice, and I know them, and they follow me" (John 10:27). Through quiet times in the presence of the

Lord, I can learn to recognize His voice. The Word of God reveals, "Thou wilt keep him in perfect peace, whose mind is stayed on thee: because he trusteth in thee" (Isa. 26:3). Therefore, I will trust in the Lord forever and keep my mind stayed on Him, always seeking quiet times alone with Him.

Related Scriptures: *Psalms 37:7; Isaiah 26:3; Matthew 11:28; John 10:14; John 10:27.*

Prayer: O Lord, I love you and I know you love me. Thank you for the confidence, peace, rest, and trust that come as I quiet my heart before you.

Affirmation: "There is a place of quiet rest near to the heart of God" (Cleland B. McAffee).

REBELLION

Commitment: By God's grace I will never again rebel against the Lord.

Scripture for Today: *"For rebellion is as the sin of witchcraft, and stubbornness is as iniquity and idolatry"* (1 Sam. 15:23).

Quote of the Day: "The devil's helpers lurk nearby when seeds of rebellion are sown" (Clift Richards).

Meditation: When I read the words, "... rebellion is as the sin of witchcraft, ..." I begin to realize how serious a matter this is to God. God wants me to obey Him in all things, to walk according to His Word, to willingly follow Him, and this I will do with the help of His Spirit in my life. Throughout this day I will endeavor to live out the meaning of the hymn, "Trust and Obey." I believe the hymn-writer's counsel: "Trust and obey, for there's no other way to be happy in Jesus, but to trust and obey" (James H. Sammis). Samuel, the prophet, concurs: "To obey is better than sacrifice . . ." (1 Sam. 15:22).

Related Scriptures: *1 Samuel 15:22; Isaiah 1:20; Romans 6:13.*

Prayer: Lord, I will walk with you today. I will walk in the light of your Word. Where you send me I will go. What you speak to me I will do.

Affirmation: I delight in obeying God. (See Ps. 40:8.)

RELATIONSHIP WITH GOD

Commitment: By God's grace I will never again blame the Lord for my mistakes.

Scripture for Today: *"For the law of the Spirit of life in Christ Jesus hath made me free from the law of sin and death"* (Rom. 8:2).

Quote of the Day: "To what extent does my religion affect my life? What does it do for me, outwardly, inwardly? What changes, transformations in attitudes, habits, personality have been wrought?" (Anonymous).

Meditation: I will take personal responsibility for my choices. I will never again try to shift the blame for my mistakes, sins, and errors onto God or other people. I will grow under the responsibilities God gives to me, and I will learn from my mistakes. I know that this will involve repentance, and I like how a small girl once defined this "big word": "It's being sorry enough to quit." It is God's goodness in my life that leads me to repentance (See Rom. 2:4), and I will let His goodness restore me as I repent of my sins and become a responsible individual under Him.

Related Scriptures: *Romans 2:4; 2 Corinthians 7:10; Ephesians 4:22-24.*

Prayer: Lord, thank you for showing me the importance of my relationship with you. I want to cultivate intimacy with you throughout this day by meditating upon your Word, obeying you, practicing your presence, and being truly repentant when I do wrong.

Affirmation: I am renewed by God's righteousness and holiness.

RELATIONSHIPS
WITH OTHERS

Commitment: By God's grace I will never again choose not to forgive when I am wronged.

Scripture for Today: *"If ye forgive not men their trespasses, neither will your Father forgive your trespasses"* (Matt. 6:15).

Quote of the Day: "Humanity is never so beautiful as when praying for forgiveness, or else forgiving another" (Jean Paul Richter).

Meditation: Mark Twain wrote, "Forgiveness is the fragrance the violet sheds on the heel that has crushed it." I want the fragrance of forgiveness to permeate all my relationships. God has forgiven me of my sins; therefore, I should forgive others. I will walk in love and forgiveness throughout this day because I know this is God's will for me. When Peter asked the Lord how often he should forgive his brother, Jesus replied, "I say not unto thee, Until seven times: but, Until seventy times seven" (Matt. 18:22). The multiplication gives us a total of 490 times, but I know that my Christian commitment requires me to go beyond even that number in the times I forgive those who do me wrong.

Related Scriptures: *Matthew 6:14; Matthew 18:21-22; Colossians 3:13.*

Prayer: Father, I want to obey your Word which tells me, "And be ye kind one to another, tenderhearted, forgiving one another, even as God for Christ's sake hath forgiven you" (Eph. 4:32).

Affirmation: I will practice the loving art of forgiveness today.

SAFETY

Commitment: By God's grace I will never again reject the Lord's protection in my life.

Scripture for Today: *"But the Lord is faithful, who shall stablish you, and keep you from evil"* (2 Thess. 3:3).

Quote of the Day: "Life is either a daring adventure, or nothing" (Helen Keller).

Meditation: Jude 24 is often used as a benediction. This is a good practice, because this passage is truly a benediction for my life: "Now unto him that is able to keep you from falling, and to present you faultless before the presence of his glory with exceeding joy. To the only wise God our Saviour, be glory and majesty, dominion and power, both now and ever. Amen." I believe this promise from God's Word, and I receive it for my life today. My God is able — He is able to keep me from falling, to establish and protect me (See 1 Pet. 5:10), to keep my heart and mind through Christ Jesus (See Phil. 4:7). God is my high tower (See Ps. 144:2), my place of refuge (See Ps. 62:8), my fortress (See Ps. 31:3), my rock (See Ps. 18:2), and my sure defense (See Ps. 62:2). I am completely safe in Him.

Related Scriptures: *Psalms 18:2; Psalms 31:3; Psalms 62:2; Psalms 62:8; Psalms 144:2; Romans 8:38-39; Philippians 4:7; 1 Peter 5:10; Jude 24.*

Prayer: Father, thank you for protecting me at all times. You are my light and my salvation and I shall not fear. (See Ps. 27:1.)

Affirmation: I am completely safe in Jesus.

SALVATION

Commitment: By God's grace I will never again forget the Lord's great work of salvation in my life.

Scripture for Today: *"Therefore if any man be in Christ, he is a new creature: old things are passed away; behold, all things are become new"* (2 Cor. 5:17).

Quote of the Day: "We are saved by someone doing for us what we cannot do for ourselves" (Donald Lester).

Meditation: Jesus came to seek and to save that which was lost. (See Matt. 18:11.) I was a lost sheep without a shepherd until Jesus came to find me. Now He has become my Good Shepherd. (See John 10:11.) He gave His life for me, and I am now His. He knows me by name, and I know Him. (See John 10:11-14.)

Jesus came to give me life — a life that is more abundant than life in this world could ever be. (See John 10:10.) He has saved me from myself, death, sin, shame, and fear. Hallelujah! What a Savior!

Related Scriptures: *Matthew 18:11; John 3:16; John 10:10-14; Ephesians 2:8-9.*

Prayer: Thank you, Father, for sending Jesus to be the sacrifice for my sins. (See 1 John 2:2.) He is perfecting His work of salvation in my life.

Affirmation: Jesus is my Savior.

SEEKING GOD

Commitment: By God's grace I will never stop seeking the Lord.

Scripture for Today: *"Seek the Lord, and his strength: seek his face evermore"* (Ps. 105:4).

Quote of the Day: "A seeking heart always finds the truth" (Anonymous).

Meditation: "And it came to pass, that as he was come nigh unto Jericho, a certain blind man sat by the way side begging: And hearing the multitude pass by, he asked what it meant. And they told him, that Jesus of Nazareth passeth by. And he cried, saying, Jesus, thou Son of David, have mercy on me . . ." (Luke 18:35-38). This blind man was understandably desperate. He called and cried out for help. He joined his need with his faith and with his quest. He was not about to be dissuaded. He put everything he had into reaching his goal — to be made whole. Jesus honored his faith and said, "Receive thy sight: thy faith hath saved thee" (Luke 18:42). The Bible says, "And immediately he received his sight" (Luke 18:43). I will follow the example of this blind man throughout this day. I will join my faith with my quest for all God has in store for me, and I know He will come through for me as He did for the blind man of Jericho.

Related Scriptures: *Psalms 40:16; Psalms 42:1; Proverbs 8:17; Luke 18:35-43.*

Prayer: Lord, I seek you with all my heart, mind, and strength. As the deer pants after the brooks of water so does my heart pant for you. (See Ps. 42:1.)

Affirmation: I will keep on seeking God.

SERVING GOD

Commitment: By God's grace I will never again forget that Jesus has chosen me to bear lasting fruit.

Scripture for Today: *"Ye have not chosen me, but I have chosen you, and ordained you, that ye should go and bring forth fruit, and that your fruit should remain: that whatsoever ye shall ask of the Father in my name, he may give it you"* (John 15:16).

Quote of the Day: "Life is like a game of tennis; the player who serves well seldom loses" (Anonymous).

Meditation: Jesus chose me so that I would go forth in service and bear lasting fruit for Him. This is my purpose and my goal. I realize that I cannot serve both God and materialism (See Matt. 6:24), therefore, I will focus on serving

God and serving others. In this way I will bear fruit for the Master. Service is love made visible, and I want to bear the fruit of love in all my relationships and responsibilities. (See Gal. 5:22.) I know the end result of my service to Christ will be His approval: "Well done, thou good and faithful servant: thou hast been faithful over a few things, I will make thee ruler over many things: enter thou into the joy of thy lord" (Matt. 25:21). I am happy in the service of the King, and I look forward to hearing Him say those words to me.

Related Scriptures: *Matthew 6:24; Matthew 25:21; John 15:5; 1 Corinthians 7:20; Galatians 5:22.*

Prayer: Lord, thank you for choosing me to bear lasting fruit in your name. This I will do with the help of your Holy Spirit.

Affirmation: I am a fruitful Christian.

SIMPLICITY

Commitment: By God's grace I will never again permit my life to become more complicated than necessary.

Scripture for Today: *"For our rejoicing is this, the testimony of our conscience, that in simplicity and godly sincerity, not with fleshly wisdom, but by the grace of God, we have had our conversation in the world, and more abundantly to you-ward"* (2 Cor. 1:12).

Quote of the Day: "I am always content with what happens; for I know that what God chooses is better than what I choose" (Epictetus).

Meditation: It is clear that God wants me to simplify my life insofar as I am able to do so. Overcomplicating one's life is a corruption of God's purpose. Simple faith, simple obedience, simple trust — these are God's will for me. Such simplicity leads to contentment which is one of life's richest treasures. I will remember the words of Sir James Mackintosh: "It is right to be contented with what we have, but never with what we are." I am not what I hope to be, I am not what I ought to be, I am not what I want to be, but by the grace of God, I am not what I once was!

Related Scriptures: *1 Corinthians 14:33; 2 Corinthians 11:3; Philippians 4:11; Hebrews 13:5.*

Prayer: Lord, I want to hold onto the simplicity I have in Christ. As I approach life with greater simplicity, I know I will have peace. I thank you that you are the author of peace. (See 1 Cor. 14:33.)

Affirmation: I will keep my life simple and peaceful in Christ.

SIN

Commitment: By God's grace I will never again choose to walk in sin.

Scripture for Today: *"So then they that are in the flesh cannot please God"* (Rom. 8:8).

Quote of the Day: "The penalty of sin is that gradually you get used to it and do not know that it is sin" (Oswald Chambers).

Meditation: Sin separates me from God. The Bible says, "for whatsoever is not of faith is sin" (Rom. 14:23). I'll walk in faith, therefore, not in sin or in the flesh. Above all else, I want to please God, and I know, "without faith it is impossible to please him: for he that cometh to God must believe that he is, and that he is a rewarder of them that diligently seek him" (Heb. 11:6). I believe in God. I will seek Him throughout this day. I will exercise my faith in Him at every opportunity. He is my Rewarder.

Related Scriptures: *Romans 6:11; Romans 14:23; Hebrews 11:6.*

Prayer: Father, I thank you for making me dead to sin, but alive unto you through Jesus Christ, my Lord. (See Rom. 6:11.)

Affirmation: I am walking in faith.

SINCERITY

Commitment: By God's grace I will never again permit any hypocrisy to enter my life.

Scripture for Today: *"Now therefore fear the Lord, and serve him in sincerity and in truth"* (Josh. 24:14).

Quote of the Day: "There is no substitute for sincerity" (Anonymous).

Meditation: The Bible says, "Let love be without dissimulation. Abhor that which is evil; cleave to that which is good" (Rom. 12:9). The word "dissimulation" means "hypocrisy," and we are admonished to avoid it at all costs — in relationships, behavior, and every aspect of life. I choose to let my life be without dissimulation. I do abhor all evil, and I will cling to that which is good — to Jesus Christ, my Lord and Savior, His Word, and His ways. I will feed upon the "unleavened bread of sincerity and truth" (See 1 Cor. 5:7-8). I will walk in sincerity and truth in all my relationships and responsibilities of this day.

Related Scriptures: *John 8:32; John 14:6; 1 Corinthians 5:7-8.*

Prayer: Lord, you are the way, the truth, and the life. (See John 14:6.) Your truth has set me free. (See John 8:32.) I want your truth and sincerity to flow through my life to others.

Affirmation: I will let sincerity and genuineness govern my behavior.

SPIRITUALITY

Commitment: By God's grace I will never again lean upon my own understanding.

Scripture for Today: *"Trust in the Lord with all thine heart; and lean not unto thine own understanding. In all thy ways acknowledge him, and he shall direct thy paths"* (Prov. 3:5-6).

Quote of the Day: "When you have no helpers, see all your helpers in God. When you have many helpers, see God in all your helpers. When you have nothing but God, see all in God; when you have everything, see God in everything. Under all conditions, stay thy heart only on the Lord" (Charles Haddon Spurgeon).

Meditation: Trust is the foundation of all successful relationships, especially

my relationship with God. I will
approach my relationship with God
today as Hammer William Webb-Peploe
advises, "Don't try to hold God's hand;
let Him hold yours. Let Him do the
holding, and you the trusting." I will
trust God with all my heart. I will not
lean on my own understanding — the
old mind-set of the world that I used to
use to try to figure things out. I will,
"Trust in him at all times" (Ps. 62:8).

Related Scriptures: *Psalms 62:8;
Psalms 146:3; 1 Timothy 4:15.*

Prayer: Lord, I know that you are
completely trustworthy in every respect.
Your Word can be depended upon.
Therefore, I will trust you unreservedly
throughout this day.

Affirmation: I trust the Lord.

STRENGTH

Commitment: By God's grace I will never again forget that the Lord is my strength.

Scripture for Today: *"Now unto him that is able to do exceeding abundantly above all that we ask or think, according to the power that worketh in us, Unto him be glory in the church by Christ Jesus throughout all ages, world without end"* (Eph. 3:20).

Quote of the Day: "Spiritual strength is man's inheritance, the eternal power granted him at the creation. It is God's breath within him" (Angelo Patri).

Meditation: The Word of God has much to say about strength. Paul wrote that the strength of Jesus "is made perfect in weakness" (2 Cor. 12:9). The Psalmist proclaimed, "The Lord is my light and my salvation; whom shall I fear? the Lord is the strength of my life; of whom shall I be afraid?" (Ps. 27:1). Isaiah prophesied, "But they that wait upon the Lord shall renew their strength; they shall mount up with wings as eagles; they shall run, and not be weary; and they shall walk and not faint" (Isa. 40:31). In moments of weakness I will turn to the Lord's strength. I will rely upon God's strength. I will wait on the Lord in the full expectation that He will renew my strength.

Related Scriptures: *Psalms 27:1; Isaiah 40:31; 2 Corinthians 12:9; Ephesians 3:17-19.*

Prayer: O Lord, you are my strength. I will lean on you.

Affirmation: I am strong in the Lord.

STRESS

Commitment: By God's grace I will never again let worry dominate my thoughts.

Scripture for Today: *"Casting all your care upon him; for he careth for you"* (1 Pet. 5:7).

Quote of the Day: "Yield not in trouble to dismay. God can deliver any day" (Martin Luther).

Meditation: Someone wrote, quite accurately, "Worry affects circulation, the heart, the glands, the whole nervous system. I have never known a man who died from overwork, but many who died from doubt" (Charles H. Mayo). Jesus said, "Thou art . . . troubled about many things: but one thing is needful" (Luke 10:41-42). That one needful thing is building a close, personal relationship with Him. This is my choice for today, and always — I will draw closer and closer to my Lord. James wrote, "Draw nigh to God, and he will draw nigh to you" (James 4:8). This is a spiritual principle that cannot fail. It has the power to dissipate all the stress in my life.

Related Scriptures: *Luke 10:41-42; Colossians 3:15; James 4:8.*

Prayer: Lord, as I draw close to you I sense you drawing close to me, and knowing you are there with me is the greatest stress-reducer in the world.

Affirmation: No worry — no fear!

TEMPERANCE (SELF-CONTROL)

Commitment: By God's grace I will never again let my flesh have preeminence in my life.

Scripture for Today: *"But put ye on the Lord Jesus Christ, and make not provision for the flesh, to fulfil the lusts thereof"* (Rom. 13:14).

Quote of the Day: "Temperance is moderation in the things that are good and total abstinence from the things that are foul" (Frances E. Willard).

Meditation: Benjamin Franklin wrote, "Temperance puts wood on the fire, meal in the barrel, flour in the tub, money in the purse, credit in the country, contentment in the house, clothes on the children, vigor in the body, intelligence in the brain, and spirit in the whole constitution." I will walk in temperance today because I know it will have good effects in my body, soul, and spirit. Temperance, in fact, is a fruit of the Holy Spirit in my life: "But the fruit of the Spirit is love, joy, peace, longsuffering, gentleness, goodness, faith, meekness, temperance: against such there is no law" (Gal. 5:22-23).

Related Scriptures: *Luke 9:23-25; Galatians 5:22-23.*

Prayer: Father, help me to keep my flesh, mind, emotions, and will under control throughout this day. Fill me with your Spirit so that I will bear the fruit of temperance in all my relationships and responsibilities. (See Gal. 5:22-23.)

Affirmation: I will control my mind, emotions, and body throughout this day.

THANKSGIVING

Commitment: By God's grace I will never again forget the importance of being thankful.

Scripture for Today: *"Offer unto God thanksgiving; and pay thy vows unto the most High"* (Ps. 50:14).

Quote of the Day: "Thanksgiving is nothing if not a glad and reverent lifting of the heart to God in honour and praise for His goodness" (James R. Miller).

Meditation: The Bible says, "It is a good thing to give thanks unto the Lord" (Ps. 92:1). As I reflect upon the truth of this verse, I realize that thanksgiving is a good thing for several reasons: it changes my perspective, it lifts my heart, it draws me close to God, it erases all negativity, it is healthy, and it is an obedient response to the Word of God. Throughout this day, therefore, I will "give thanks unto the Lord, for he is good: for his mercy endureth for ever" (Ps. 107:1).

Related Scriptures: *1 Chronicles 16:8; Psalms 26:7; Psalms 92:1; Psalms 107:1; Psalms 116:17.*

Prayer: Father, I thank you for all you have done for me, and I thank you for who you are. Throughout this day I will count my blessings because I know you have been very good to me.

Affirmation: My heart overflows with thanksgiving to God.

THINGS

Commitment: By God's grace I will never again let things — or anything — come between me and my Lord.

Scripture for Today: *"But seek ye first the kingdom of God, and his righteousness; and all these things shall be added unto you"* (Matt. 6:33).

Quote of the Day: "The wise man carries his possessions within him" (Bias of Priene).

Meditation: I live in an age of materialism, but I do not want materialistic values to infect me. I want to obey Jesus who said, "Lay not up for yourselves treasures upon earth, where moth and rust doth corrupt, and where thieves break through and steal: But lay up for yourselves treasures in heaven, where neither moth nor rust doth corrupt, and where thieves do not break through nor steal: For where your treasure is, there will your heart be also" (Matt. 6:19-21). I want my treasures to be spiritual ones, not material things.

Related Scriptures: *Psalms 27:3-4; Psalms 37:4; Matthew 6:19-21; Ephesians 1:3.*

Prayer: Lord, thank you for the treasures I possess in you. You have blessed me with every spiritual blessing in Christ Jesus, and I'd rather have those blessings than anything this world has to offer. (See Eph. 1:3.)

Affirmation: I'd rather have Jesus than anything else.

UNCERTAINTY

Commitment: By God's grace I will never again lose sight of the fact that God is at work in my life.

Scripture for Today: *"Being confident of this very thing, that he which hath begun a good work in you will perform it until the day of Jesus Christ"* (Phil. 1:6).

Quote of the Day: "The greatest of all certainties is uncertainty" (Anonymous).

Meditation: As a follower of Jesus Christ, I have no uncertainties except those I permit myself to entertain. Though I can't always be certain about everything, I can be certain that God is in charge, that He knows what is best for me, and that He is working things out in my life according to His purpose. His Word is a book of certainty. With Him, I know my future is secure. Therefore, I will not worry about the uncertainties that confront me. I will believe that God will work everything out in my behalf.

Related Scriptures: *Romans 8:28; Hebrews 10:35-36.*

Prayer: Lord, thank you for the certainty in my life that comes through faith. I will always be confident that you will fulfill your promises in my life.

Affirmation: I am a confident believer.

VALOR

Commitment: By God's grace I will never again shrink back in the face of challenges.

Scripture for Today: *"Wait on the Lord: be of good courage, and he shall strengthen thine heart: wait, I say, on the Lord"* (Ps. 27:14).

Quote of the Day: "Courage is holding on a minute longer" (General George S. Patton).

Meditation: Many military men have spoken about courage because courage is a necessary attribute in time of war. One of these was General Douglas MacArthur who said, "Last, but by no means least, courage — moral courage, the courage of one's convictions, the courage to see things through. The world is in a constant conspiracy against the brave. It's the age-old struggle — the roar of the crowd on one side and the voice of your conscience on the other." I will follow the voice of my conscience throughout this day, and I know God will bless me.

Related Scriptures: *Deuteronomy 33:27; 1 Corinthians 16:13.*

Prayer: Lord, you have given me the courage I need to face all challenges. Thank you for always being there with me.

Affirmation: I am courageous through faith in Christ.

WISDOM

Commitment: By God's grace I will never again fail to realize that the Bible is my source for wisdom.

Scripture for Today: *"Thy testimonies are wonderful: therefore doth my soul keep them. The entrance of thy words giveth light; it giveth understanding unto the simple"* (Ps. 119:129-130).

Quote of the Day: "I know the Bible is inspired because it inspires me" (Dwight L. Moody).

Meditation: The Bible is a promise-book from my heavenly Father to me. I receive each of its promises with faith. I greatly enjoy meditating upon Psalms 119 which talks about God's Word. This chapter tells me to walk in the Word of God, to take heed to it, to memorize it, to meditate upon it, to run with it, to delight myself in its commandments, and to walk in the light it sheds upon my pathway. This I will do because I know the results will include happiness, cleansing from sin, no shame, blessings, enlightenment, wisdom, and life. I love the Word of God and the wisdom it imparts to me.

Related Scriptures: *Psalms 33:6; Psalms 119; Romans 10:8-9; Hebrews 4:12.*

Prayer: Lord, thank you for your Word. I will meditate upon its precepts throughout this day, and I will walk in the light it sheds upon my pathway.

Affirmation: God imparts His wisdom to me through His Word.

BOOK ORDER FORM

Use this form to order additional copies of this book or for more information about other inspirational books.

Book Title	Price	Quantity	Amount
By God's Grace Volume I	$ 6.99	______	$ ______
*Shipping & Handling — Add $2.00 for the **first** book, **plus** $0.50 for **each** additional book.*			$ ______
TOTAL ORDER AMOUNT *— Enclose check or money order. (No cash or C.O.D.'s.)*			$ ______

☐ Please send me information on other inspirational books.

☐ SPECIAL CHURCH DISCOUNT for orders of 50 or more call **1-800-495-5577**.

Make check or money order payable to: **GATEWAY INTERNATIONAL.**
Mail order to: **Gateway International**
P.O Box 702008
Tulsa, OK 74170

Please print your name and address **clearly:**

Name ______________________________

Address ______________________________

City ______________________________

State or Province ______________________________

Zip or Postal Code ______________________________

Telephone Number (____) ______________________________

Foreign orders must be submitted by Credit Card only. Additional shipping costs will apply. Foreign orders are shipped by uninsured surface mail. We ship all orders within 48 hours of receipt of order.

MasterCard or VISA — For credit card orders you may use your MasterCard or VISA by completing the following information, or for **faster service,** call **1-800-495-5577**.

Card Name ______________________________

Card Number ______________________________

Expiration Date ______________________________

Signature ______________________________

(authorized signature)

Cut here